Cuando Sea Grande / When I Grow Up

PUEDO SER UN JUGADOR DE FÚTBOL/ I CAN BE A FOOTBALL PLAYER

By Alex Appleby   Traducido por Eida de la Vega

Gareth Stevens
PUBLISHING

Please visit our website, www.garethstevens.com. For a free color catalog of all our high-quality books, call toll free 1-800-542-2595 or fax 1-877-542-2596.

Library of Congress Cataloging-in-Publication Data

I can be a football player = Puedo ser un jugador de fútbol / by Alex Appleby, translated by Eida de la Vega.
p. cm. — (When I grow up = Cuando sea grande)
Parallel title: Cuando sea grande
In English and Spanish.
Includes index.
ISBN 978-1-4824-0859-1 (library binding)
1. Football — Vocational guidance — Juvenile literature. 2. Football — Juvenile literature. 3. Football players — Juvenile literature. I. Appleby, Alex. II. Title.
GV950.7 A66 2015
796.33—d23

First Edition

Published in 2015 by
Gareth Stevens Publishing
111 East 14th Street, Suite 349
New York, NY 10003

Copyright © 2015 Gareth Stevens Publishing

Editor: Ryan Nagelhout
Designer: Sarah Liddell
Spanish Translation: Eida de la Vega

Photo credits: Cover, p. 1 (player) Steven Leon Day/Shutterstock.com; cover, p. 1 (field) Joseph W. Pyle/Shutterstock.com; p. 5 Natalya Gerasimova/iStock/Thinkstock.com; p. 7 4736202690/Shutterstock.com; pp. 9, 24 (throw) Robert Kelsey/iStock/Thinkstock.com; pp. 11, 24 (throw) Monkey Business Images/Monkey Business/Thinkstock.com; p. 13 SUSAN LEGGETT/Shutterstock.com; pp. 15, 17, 19 Yellow Dog Productions/The Image Bank/Getty Images; p. 21 Brand X Pictures/Stockbyte/Thinkstock.com; pp. 23, 24 (football) Comstock/Stockbyte/Thinkstock.com.

Printed in the United States of America

CPSIA compliance information: Batch #CS15GS: For further information contact Gareth Stevens, New York, New York at 1-800-542-2595.

Contenido

Contents

Me encanta jugar fútbol americano.

I love to play football.

Cuando sea grande
quiero jugar
al fútbol americano.

I want to play
when I grow up.

Me encanta correr
con el balón.

I love to run
with the football.

También lanzo el balón.

I throw the ball, too.

Me gusta ser
mariscal de campo.

I like to
play quarterback.

Juego con mis amigos.

I play with my friends.

¡Anotamos
un *touchdown*!

We scored
a touchdown!

Es divertido ganar.

It is fun to win games.

Me entreno
para ser mejor.
Eso se llama práctica.

I work hard
to get better.
This is called practice.

¡Un día seré
jugador profesional!

One day I will be
a pro!

23

Palabras que debes saber/ Words to Know

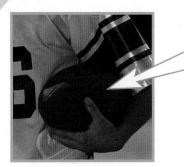

(el) balón/
football

correr/
run

lanzar/
throw

Índice/Index

24